I0704751

Jean Baptiste Willermoz
Founder of Authentic Freemasonry

Jacques Florent Di Gubbio

Jean Baptiste Willermoz
Founder of Authentic Freemasonry

Historical Test

ISBN : 9798343103922
Publisher : Independently published
Legal deposit : on publication

Preface

This book was born of a profound desire to pay tribute to an emblematic yet often overlooked figure in the history of Freemasonry : Jean-Baptiste Willermoz. Through his exceptional career, his bold reforms and his spiritual vision, Willermoz played a central role in building authentic Masonry, rooted in a quest for truth and reintegration of the soul. He is the founder of the Rectified Scottish Regime, a form of Freemasonry that continues to inspire thousands of Freemasons around the world with its spiritual depth and initiatory teachings. At a time when French society, and more broadly European society, was undergoing great intellectual and social upheaval, Willermoz bridged the gap between the ideals of the Enlightenment and the esoteric and mystical currents that were gaining in influence. This book attempts to retrace not only his personal itinerary, but also to decipher the lasting influence he exerted on modern Masonry. It is essential to place his actions and reforms in the context of the 18th century, when religious, philosophical and spiritual ideas were in ferment. My aim through these pages is to provide a rigorous and accessible look at Willermoz's life, shedding light on his career, his decisive encounters, and above all, the impact of his work on contemporary Freemasonry. This book is not only a biography, but also a reflection on how a man was able to combine Christian spirituality, Masonic initiation and mystical commitment to profoundly transform an institution which, even today, continues to evolve under the influence of his teachings. Modern Freemasonry, as we know it, owes much of its richness and spiritual depth to reformers like Jean-Baptiste Willermoz. The aim of this book is to fully rehabilitate Willermoz, demonstrating that he was one of the true architects of authentic Freemasonry, focused on the quest for spiritual reintegration and moral perfection. It is with this analytical framework that I invite you to dive into this book, to discover or rediscover the life and work of this remarkable man, and to explore how his ideas continue to resonate in today's Masonic lodges.

Jacques Florent Di Gubbio

Introduction

Jean-Baptiste Willermoz, a key figure in the history of 18th-century Freemasonry, left an indelible mark on this initiatory society. Founder of the Rectified Scottish Regime (RSR), he reformed and reoriented Freemasonry to make it a true spiritual path, faithful to esoteric and Christian traditions. But to understand the importance of his work, it is necessary to place Willermoz in the context of his time, when mystical, religious and philosophical ideas were in full ferment. This introduction aims to provide an overview of the historical and social context in which Willermoz evolved, to analyze the religious influences that nourished his thought, and finally to lay the foundations for this work, which seeks to demonstrate the central role played by this man in the formation of modern, so-called "authentic" Freemasonry. The 18th century, the Age of Enlightenment, was a period of political, social and intellectual upheaval. In France, it marked the rise of a triumphant rationalism, embodied by thinkers such as Voltaire, Diderot and Rousseau, who criticized traditional institutions, notably the Catholic Church and absolute monarchy. This rise of the Enlightenment was accompanied by a quest for liberty, equality and fraternity that culminated in the French Revolution of 1789. However, alongside this rationalist movement, another equally influential but less visible trend was developing : Christian esotericism and mysticism. In this context, Freemasonry played a central role. It attracted men of letters, philosophers, members of the nobility and the enlightened bourgeoisie, seduced by its ideals of fraternity, tolerance and the search for truth. Freemasonry, as it existed in the 18th century, offered a framework for the encounter between the philosophical ideas of the Enlightenment and a deeper spiritual quest. However, Freemasonry itself was undergoing a profound transformation. Initially focused on philosophical and social concerns, it was evolving towards a more esoteric initiatory quest. It was in this context that Jean-Baptiste Willermoz was to play a decisive role. Born in Lyon in 1730, Willermoz grew up in a society marked by a religiosity that was still very much present, but in the throes of change. Lyon, a city of enlightened merchants and bourgeoisie, was also a major center of esoteric and mystical thought. Initiatic societies flourished there, attracting men in search of meaning and truth. It was in this environment that Willermoz took his first steps in Freemasonry, initiated in 1750 at the age of 20 in a Lyon lodge. He quickly established himself as a key figure in Lyon's Masonic milieu, as well as a visionary reformer. Jean-Baptiste Willermoz did not arrive at Freemasonry and his concept of Christian, mystical and reforming Masonry by chance.

His intellectual and spiritual path was marked by several major influences, which were to crystallize in his work of reform. Among these influences, Pietism occupies a central place. Originating in Germany in the 17th century, Pietism advocated a return to a personal, intimate faith, based on the reading of Scripture, prayer and the quest for an irreproachable moral life. This Protestant reform movement is distinguished by its rejection of ritual formality and its insistence on a direct relationship with God. Although Willermoz was a Catholic, he was strongly influenced by this idea of a personal, intimate relationship with the divine, outside rigid institutional structures. Secondly, it's impossible to understand Willermoz's thought without mentioning the influence of Christian theosophy, an esoteric movement that seeks to penetrate the mysteries of God and creation through intuitive, mystical knowledge. Christian theosophy, developed in particular by thinkers such as Jacob Böhme, teaches that man is a divine creature, fallen from his original state through sin, and that he must undertake a path of spiritual reintegration to regain his union with God. This concept of reintegration, central to Willermoz's thinking, has its roots in this theosophical tradition. For him, Freemasonry was not just a place for fraternal encounters, but also a space where initiates could undertake this path to redemption. Finally, the initiatory societies of the 18th century, of which Willermoz was a member, had a profound influence on his vision of Freemasonry. Among these, the Ordre des Élus Coëns, founded by

Martinez de Pasqually, played a crucial role. This mystical order advocated a complex Christian theosophy, based on the idea that humanity, because of original sin, was separated from God and had to undertake a series of initiations and rituals to reintegrate itself into the divine order. Willermoz, a disciple of Pasqually, took up this idea of reintegration, which he would later integrate into the Rectified Scottish Regime. However, he added a more accessible dimension, while retaining the spiritual depth of the Coëns Chosen teachings. One of the main aims of this book is to show that Jean-Baptiste Willermoz is not only an important figure in Freemasonry, but also a reformer of the first order, who restored to Freemasonry a spiritual depth it was in danger of losing. In the 18th century, Freemasonry, influenced by the Enlightenment, tended to focus increasingly on social and philosophical concerns, to the detriment of its initiatory and mystical dimension. Willermoz, aware of this danger, set out to reform the society and return it to its original essence : a path of spiritual initiation, aimed at purifying the soul and reintegrating man into the divine order. The aim of this book is to show how Willermoz, inspired by the mystical and esoteric teachings of his time, adapted these ideas and integrated them into a structured Masonic framework, giving birth to the Rectified Scottish Regime. This initiatory system, founded in 1778 at the Lyon Convent, is based on deep-rooted Christian values and proposes a multi-degree path, with each stage corresponding to a purification and spiritual elevation. The RSR, as conceived by Willermoz, is not just a branch of Freemasonry, but a complete initiatory path, where symbolic initiation is merely a prelude to profound inner transformation. Willermoz saw Freemasonry as a tool to help people purify themselves and draw closer to God, by following the teachings of Christ. His work is therefore that of a man who wanted to give Freemasonry authenticity and spiritual depth, far removed from profane or purely philosophical concerns. In rehabilitating the Christian dimension of Freemasonry, Willermoz also opposed a certain tendency of Freemasonry to detach itself from established religions in favor of a more general deism. For him, Freemasonry cannot do without the message of Christ, which lies at the heart of the process of spiritual reintegration. The initiatory path proposed by the Rectified Scottish Regime is above all a path of return to God, through the model of Christ and the purification of the soul. This book also sets out to demonstrate that Jean-Baptiste Willermoz's influence extends far beyond the boundaries of Lyonnais Freemasonry. His Rectified Scottish Regime has survived the centuries and taken root in several European countries, where it continues to exist today. It has become a model of spiritual Freemasonry, focused on the quest for truth and the reintegration of man into divine unity.

I. Childhood and education of Jean-Baptiste Willermoz

Jean-Baptiste Willermoz was born on July 10, 1730 in Lyon, into a modest but respected family in this great industrial city. His father, Antoine Willermoz, was a silk master, a prestigious trade in Lyon, then a European center for the silk trade. His mother, Jeanne Bernard, looked after their many children. Jean-Baptiste, the eldest of fifteen siblings, quickly took on the great responsibility of helping his parents keep the family home in balance. These early years, marked by the example of hard work and family devotion, would have a profound impact on his character and the way he approached his future endeavors, both Masonic and spiritual. When Jean-Baptiste was growing up, Lyon was not just a major commercial center. It was also a crossroads of ideas, philosophical, scientific and religious. Various intellectual currents flowed through the city : the rationalism of the Enlightenment, the mystical and devout movements of the Catholic Reformation, and esoteric and alchemical ideas from Europe. Thanks to its geographical position between France, Switzerland and Italy, Lyon saw the circulation not only of goods, but also of ideas, sometimes subversive, sometimes enlightening. The Willermoz family, though economically modest, were no strangers to this environment. Church attendance, discussions with other shopkeepers and craftsmen, and public readings, especially of newspapers and pamphlets, provided fertile intellectual ground for an inquisitive young mind like Jean-Baptiste's. Very early on, he was exposed to spiritual reflections that questioned dogma and sought to reconcile reason and faith, tradition and spiritual renewal. These circumstances would influence his future attraction to Freemasonry, which he perceived as a space for spiritual freedom and the quest for truth. Despite the intellectual wealth of his environment, Jean-Baptiste's day-to-day reality was primarily that of a craftsman's son destined to follow in his father's footsteps. He quickly entered the world of work and began an apprenticeship in the silk trade. In those days, vocational training was not exclusively technical; it was accompanied by strict values of discipline, rigor and dedication to work. The values instilled in him by his father, such as honesty, perseverance and organization, were to become essential traits of Jean-Baptiste's personality. However, his education was not limited to the professional sphere. Although his formal education was probably sketchy, Willermoz developed an early taste for reading and study. He avidly read the works available to him, particularly those dealing with philosophy, religion and history. This reading, often self-taught, was the sign of an intellectual curiosity that would never leave him. At a time when the education of young boys in his milieu was generally limited to the rudiments of writing, reading and arithmetic, Jean-Baptiste stood out for his willingness to go beyond the usual knowledge of his time. He also drew on the Catholic tradition of Lyons, which had a strong influence on his upbringing, to instill values of charity and moral elevation that would leave a deep imprint on him. From an early age, Jean-Baptiste Willermoz felt an attraction to spiritual matters. In 18th-century France, the Catholic religion held a predominant place, but more personal mystical currents were also emerging. These currents, such as pietism and neo-gnostic ideas, encouraged a search for individual spirituality, a deepening of faith beyond formal religious practices. For a young man like Willermoz, driven by a quest for truth and meaning, these ideas are a call to inner action, personal transformation and the search for a wisdom hidden behind the appearances of the material world. It was in this context that he first read mystical and esoteric texts dealing with man's reintegration into his original state, a central theme that would run through all his future work. Strongly influenced by theories of redemption and spiritual regeneration, he began to perceive life as an initiatory journey, a series of trials designed to turn human beings into channels of divine light. It was in this environment of intellectual and spiritual ferment that Jean-Baptiste Willermoz was initiated into Freemasonry in 1750, at the age of 20. At the time, Freemasonry was still a relatively new institution in France, and its lodges attracted men in search of knowledge, intellectual emancipation and brotherhood. In Lyon, as in other major cities, lodges were meeting places for men of diverse backgrounds, united by a desire to explore new ideas and deepen their understanding of human and divine nature. Willermoz was initiated into La Parfaite Amitié, a relatively new Masonic lodge, but already influential in Lyon. The experience of this initiation was a real turning point for him. He discovered a structured framework for his spiritual quest, a place where esoteric symbolism enriched his personal reflections. He soon became involved in lodge activities and established himself as a respected member, thanks to his seriousness, willingness to learn and natural charisma. Through Freemasonry, Willermoz came into contact with other men sharing the same intellectual and spiritual concerns. He also discovered the complexity and richness of Masonic rites, which, in his eyes, were not mere social ceremonies, but tools for genuine inner work. These first steps in Masonry confirmed his vision of life as a path of initiation. However, he already sensed that the Freemasonry of his time was incomplete and could go further in his quest for spiritual reintegration. This realization would later lead him to radically reform Freemasonry through the creation of the Rectified Scottish Regime. Beyond Freemasonry, Willermoz found in his professional life principles that would also shape his approach to Masonic spirituality and organization. The profession of master silk-maker, with its demand for precision, rigor and patience, forged in him a keen sense of discipline. In the family workshop, he learned the importance of detail, the need to plan each step carefully, and humility in the face of the constant effort required to create a finished work. This discipline of mind and body translates naturally into his approach to masonry. Just as a master craftsman works to perfect his art, Willermoz sees the Freemason as an apprentice in the art of living and thinking. He sees Masonic progression through the ranks as a metaphor for inner perfection, where each step is a test to be overcome, each degree a new understanding to be acquired. The parallel between craftsmanship and Masonic initiation would become central to his thinking. For him, to be a Freemason is first and foremost to be a craftsman of oneself, someone who shapes one's own being in accordance with the principles of truth, justice and fraternity. It was in this spirit that he would later develop his Masonic reforms, seeking to give the rites a deeper meaning and linking them directly to spiritual elevation. From an early age, Willermoz displayed a certain natural authority. As the eldest of fifteen children, he developed management and decision-making skills at an early age. This family experience reinforced his ability to organize, lead and unite people around him. At La Parfaite Amitié lodge, his leadership qualities were quickly recognized. His seriousness, wisdom and mastery of Masonic ideas make him a role model for the other brothers. This leadership temperament is expressed not only in his ability to lead, but also in his willingness to reform. Willermoz was not a man to settle for existing structures if he felt they were imperfect. This aspiration to improve what can be improved will never leave him.

II. First steps in Freemasonry

In 1750, at the age of twenty, Jean-Baptiste Willermoz made a choice that would profoundly influence the rest of his life : he joined Freemasonry. This decision was not insignificant in the context of 18th-century France. Freemasonry, then in full expansion, was still shrouded in mystery and suspicion. For a young man from Lyon, a city marked by intellectual, mystical and religious currents, this initiation was both an act of intellectual curiosity and an opening onto a wider spiritual world. However, for Willermoz, this first contact with Freemasonry was much more than a simple affiliation to a secret society : it was the beginning of an initiatory journey that would lead him to become one of Freemasonry's most influential reformers. Jean-Baptiste Willermoz was initiated into Freemasonry in his native Lyon. He joined La Parfaite Amitié lodge, one of the first Masonic lodges founded in the city. Freemasonry in Lyons was still in its infancy. La Parfaite Amitié lodge, founded shortly before Willermoz's arrival, was affiliated to the Grand Orient de France, the country's main Masonic obedience. Like other French lodges, it attracted a wide range of men : merchants, craftsmen, intellectuals, lawyers and members of the local aristocracy. For Jean-Baptiste, the lodge represents an opportunity to connect with other individuals who share a common quest for truth, brotherhood and moral perfection. The lodge is also a meeting place to discuss the new ideas circulating in Enlightenment Europe. These men, though from diverse social backgrounds, are united by a common desire to transcend the limits of class distinctions and strict religious dogma. Willermoz's initiation followed the rituals of 18th-century lodges. Masonic initiation ceremonies, imbued with symbolism and esoteric rites, left a lasting impression on him. The candidate is symbolically staged in a process of death and rebirth, symbolizing the inner transformation that Freemasonry promises to achieve. Candlelight, the geometric layout of the furniture, the use of symbols such as the compass and the square, and the words spoken during the initiation oaths create an atmosphere conducive to reflection on the profound meaning of life and human existence. For Willermoz, this initiation was more than just joining a fraternal circle : it became the starting point of a spiritual quest. He soon realized that Freemasonry was a powerful tool capable of elevating man to a moral and spiritual ideal. However, from his very first years in the lodge, he also sensed that this ideal was still incomplete in its present form. This impression would become one of the main motivations for his future commitment to reforming Freemasonry. From the moment of his initiation, Willermoz was struck by the ideals underlying Freemasonry. The rituals and symbolic teachings are all about fraternity, equality and truth.

The Masonic lodge is a place where people can meet on an equal footing, transcending social, religious and political divides. This ideal of universal brotherhood was particularly appealing to Willermoz, who saw Freemasonry as a community capable of uniting people around a common quest for self-improvement. But beyond fraternity, it was above all the aspiration to moral and spiritual perfection that attracted Jean-Baptiste Willermoz. Freemasonry in the 18th century was marked by a strong philosophical and moral dimension. Members embarked on a path of inner purification, to become better men, not only in their outward actions, but also in their innermost being. This quest for self-improvement is in keeping with the Masonic tradition of constant self-improvement, represented by the symbolism of the rough stone that the Freemason must polish to make a perfect stone. Willermoz fully embraced this idea of Freemasonry as a tool for inner transformation. He sees Masonic rites and symbols as keys to understanding the mysteries of existence and to spiritual evolution. However, although he was deeply attracted to Masonic ideals, he also felt a certain frustration : he sensed that Freemasonry as practiced in the lodges of his day lacked a deeper spiritual dimension. Philosophical and moral discussions were important, but for Willermoz, they were not enough. He was convinced that Freemasonry had to offer more than just a moral framework : it had to enable genuine spiritual regeneration of mankind. As he became more and more involved in the activities of La Parfaite Amitié lodge, Jean-Baptiste Willermoz began to feel uneasy. Although the philosophical discussions and debates on Enlightenment ideals were stimulating, he found that the Lyonnais Freemasonry of his day remained too focused on superficial aspects. Lodge meetings, sometimes transformed into mere worldly circles, seemed to him to lack the spiritual depth he sought. At the time, Freemasonry in France was experiencing a number of aberrations. In some lodges, the ideals of brotherhood and self-improvement took second place to more material concerns. Members often met for social or political reasons, and the initiatory dimension of the rites was sometimes neglected. This situation disappointed Willermoz, who saw Freemasonry as a potentially far more powerful tool for spiritual transformation. It was from these early years in the lodge that Willermoz began to consider reforms. He increasingly questioned the true meaning of Masonic rites, and how they could be redirected towards a more spiritual goal. He is convinced that Freemasonry can play a key role in the quest to reintegrate man into his original spiritual state, but for this to happen, it must rediscover its true initiatory vocation. This idea of reintegration, which was to become central to Willermoz's thinking, was largely influenced by his future encounters with mystical and esoteric thinkers. At the La Parfaite Amitié lodge, Jean-Baptiste Willermoz met several influential figures in Lyonnais masonry. These men, like himself, were driven by a quest for truth and spiritual elevation. Among them were intellectuals, theologians and practitioners of esotericism, who shared Willermoz's more spiritual vision of Freemasonry. One of the most important of these encounters was with Claude-François Achard, a learned Freemason who introduced Willermoz to esoteric and mystical ideas. Achard was deeply influenced by Christian theosophy, a spiritual movement that sought to reconcile Christian theology with esoteric ideas derived from Neoplatonism, Kabbalah and alchemy. These mystical teachings were to play a fundamental role in Willermoz's spiritual evolution. He began to perceive Freemasonry not just as a tool for moral perfection, but as an initiatory path towards the reintegration of man into the divine light. His encounter with Achard, as well as other Freemasons in Lyon, prompted Willermoz to deepen his research into Christian esotericism. He became increasingly interested in the writings of Jacob Boehme, a German mystic whose theories on the reintegration of man into his original state were to have a profound influence on Willermoz's future doctrine. Through these readings, Willermoz forged a conviction : Freemasonry must become a path of spiritual reintegration, not just a philosophical or moral debate.

III. The encounter with the Coëns Elect and the influence of Martinez de Pasqually

The decisive turning point in Jean-Baptiste Willermoz's spiritual life came in the mid-1760s, when he came into contact with the Order of the Knights Masons Elected Coëns of the Universe, founded by the mystic and theurgist Martinez de Pasqually. This encounter was to profoundly transform Willermoz's understanding of Freemasonry, spirituality and human destiny. Through this relationship, he discovered a complex esoteric vision, nourished by Christian theosophy, Hermeticism and Kabbalah, which would not only influence his beliefs, but also play a central role in the Masonic reform he would later undertake. The following pages explore this decisive encounter, the teachings of Martinez de Pasqually, and the lasting impact of these ideas on Willermoz's life and on Freemasonry. Founded in the 1760s by Martinez de Pasqually, the Ordre des Élus Coëns is a Masonic group with far higher spiritual ambitions than traditional Masonic lodges. Unlike classical Freemasonry, which focuses primarily on moral and philosophical self-improvement, the Coëns Order of the Elect is deeply rooted in mystical and gnostic theology. It aims to restore man to his original spiritual state before the Fall, by rediscovering divine purity and unity with God. Pasqually teaches that, through rigorous spiritual work, theurgical rituals and strict moral discipline, it is possible to re-establish the connection between man and the divine worlds. This approach, which blends elements of Jewish Kabbalah, Neoplatonism and mystical Christianity, quickly won Willermoz over. For him, this vision of man's reintegration into the divine light responded to his profound spiritual quest. Where traditional Freemasonry seemed to him limited in its spiritual aspirations, the Coëns Order of the Chosen offered a complete initiatory path, capable of transforming the human being from within and opening him up to divine realities. It was probably around 1765 that Jean-Baptiste Willermoz first met Martinez de Pasqually. At the time, Pasqually was already an enigmatic and charismatic figure. Born in Grenoble in 1727, he claimed to be descended from a line of theurgists who had inherited ancient secrets enabling them to communicate with higher spiritual intelligences. Mediterranean in complexion and endowed with a magnetic personality, Pasqually impressed with his vast mystical knowledge and confidence as a spiritual master. For Willermoz, meeting Pasqually was a revelation. Pasqually offered him not only answers to the spiritual questions he was asking himself, but also a concrete method for advancing along the path of divine reintegration. Through Pasqually's teachings, Willermoz discovered a much deeper understanding of Masonic symbolism. Where certain rites of Freemasonry seemed empty of meaning, Pasqually saw esoteric symbols of the fall of man and his possible redemption. Under his influence, Willermoz began to see Freemasonry not just as a philosophical society, but as a genuine school of spiritual transformation. The relationship between Pasqually and Willermoz soon became very close. Pasqually recognized in Willermoz a devoted disciple, intelligent and capable of understanding the subtleties of his esoteric teachings. As for Willermoz, he saw in Pasqually a spiritual master endowed with superior wisdom and privileged access to divine truths. This master-disciple relationship was to have a lasting influence on Willermoz's thinking, prompting him to reform Freemasonry and give it a truly spiritual and initiatory dimension. Pasqually's teachings, which he transmitted orally and through complex rituals, were based on a particular cosmogony. He teaches that man was originally a divine being, created in the image of God and endowed with considerable spiritual powers.

However, as a result of the Fall, symbolized by expulsion from the Garden of Eden, man lost his direct link with God and fell into a state of materiality. This vision of the Fall is not limited to a simple moral sin, but is seen as an ontological degradation of human nature, which has drifted away from the divine worlds and celestial light. For Pasqually, reintegrating man into his original state is possible, but requires rigorous spiritual work. This work involves moral purification, strict observance of divine laws and the practice of theurgic rituals. Through these rituals, the Coëns Elect seek to establish direct communication with higher spiritual intelligences (angels and beings of light) in order to restore divine order to the world. This theurgy, which consists in invoking the celestial powers to assist man on his path to reintegration, is at the heart of the practice of the Coëns Elect. These ideas resonated deeply with Willermoz. Since joining Freemasonry, he had been searching for a higher spiritual dimension, a way to transcend mere morality and achieve true spiritual regeneration. Pasqually's teachings offered him exactly that. He fully embraced the idea that man is on a quest to reintegrate himself into his original divine state, and that this reintegration can only be achieved through an initiatory path, involving both strict moral discipline and sophisticated ritual practice. After his meeting with

Pasqually, Jean-Baptiste Willermoz became fully involved in the Coëns Order of the Elect. He became one of the order's most active members, helping to spread Pasqually's teachings throughout France and Switzerland. As a devoted disciple, he helped set up Coëns lodges in several cities, and soon became one of Pasqually's closest collaborators. In 1767, Jean-Baptiste Willermoz was promoted to Réaux-Croix, the highest rank in the Coëns Order of the Elect. This rank, reserved for an elite group of members, implied mastery of the most advanced theurgical rituals and a thorough understanding of Pasqually's esoteric teachings. Willermoz, now at the top of the Coëns Elite hierarchy, is not only an experienced practitioner of theurgy, but also a spiritual master in the making. However, despite his total commitment to the Coëns Order, Willermoz never lost sight of his goal to reform Freemasonry. While he was convinced that Pasqually's teachings represented a pinnacle of esoteric spirituality, he also wished to make these ideas accessible to a wider public, beyond the restricted circles of the Coëns Elect. This aspiration to fuse Masonic ideals with Pasqually's mystical teachings would lead to the creation of the Rectified Scottish Regime a few years later. Although Jean-Baptiste Willermoz was deeply committed to the Coëns Order of the Elect, and regarded Martinez de Pasqually as his spiritual master, in the late 1760s he began to perceive certain limitations in the way the Order operated. The theurgical rituals, involving complex invocations and lengthy preparations, were difficult for many members to perform. Indeed, Coën theurgy demands a moral purity and rigorous discipline that are difficult to maintain over the long term. Some members of the Order, unable to follow these strict precepts, gradually drift away from ritual practices.

IV. Esoteric masonry construction in Lyon

The 18th century was a period marked by an abundance of new ideas and spiritual emergences, particularly within Freemasonry. Lyon, a city at the crossroads of many cultural and spiritual influences, became a nerve center for the flourishing of a singular esoteric Masonry, a mystical tradition on the bangs of the rationalist influences that were beginning to dominate European thought. It was against this backdrop that Jean-Baptiste Willermoz, a key figure in Lyonnais Freemasonry, set about founding La charity Lodge, with the ambition of developing a resolutely mystical and Christian Masonic path. The aim here is to trace the construction of this esoteric masonry in Lyon, exploring Willermoz's role, his relationships with other influential masonic figures such as Louis-Claude de Saint-Martin and Claude-François Achard, and their collective contribution to the development of an initiatory and spiritual tradition that transcends official Church dogma and the limits of more traditional masonry. The founding of the charity lodge in 1774 was a decisive turning point in the history of Freemasonry in Lyon. Jean-Baptiste Willermoz, a prosperous merchant and passionate Freemason, was its initiator and spiritual soul. Deeply influenced by the teachings of Martinès de Pasqually, founder of the Coëns Order of the Elect, Willermoz aspired to disseminate a Masonry in which the quest for inner enlightenment and spiritual elevation took precedence over the social and political aspects advocated by some of the century's Freemasons. Willermoz saw charity as an instrument for spreading the mystical doctrines inspired by Martinès de Pasqually and, more broadly, Christian theosophy. The lodge was to become a crucible for the teaching of occult and spiritual sciences, with a particular focus on the reintegration of man into his primordial state, an idea dear to Pasqually. Unlike some lodges more focused on moral improvement or societal reform, La charity was first and foremost a place of inner transformation, where Masonic rituals and symbols were to open the way to the regeneration of the soul. Willermoz's project was not simply a return to the spiritual sources of Christianity, but a surpassing of them, through esoteric masonry rooted in profound initiatory practices. For Willermoz, the Masonic Temple was not just a physical place, but a metaphysical space, a sacred place where spiritual operations took place, enabling the initiate to progress towards a state of superior knowledge and wisdom. La charity embodied this vision of Freemasonry as a vehicle for radical inner and spiritual transformation, far from being reduced to a mere brotherhood of men sharing humanist values. The creation of the Lyon lodge was also part of a European context in which mystical and occult currents were on the rise. The 18th century was marked by a thirst for esoteric knowledge throughout Europe. Numerous intellectuals, artists and thinkers turned to alchemy, theosophy and the Egyptian mysteries in an attempt to unlock the secrets of the universe and the human soul. Willermoz, in founding La charity, was part of this movement of spiritual research, but he did so by emphasizing a Christian initiatory path, one that aims to reintegrate man into a direct relationship with God, while drawing on ancient occult traditions. Martinès de Pasqually had a decisive influence on Willermoz. The Ordre des Élus Coëns, which he founded, was an esoteric Masonic order that combined complex ritual practices with theosophical teachings based on an esoteric Christian vision of mankind's redemption. For Pasqually, the fall of man, as described in the Bible, was not just a loss of the state of grace, but a disintegration of cosmic harmony. The role of the initiate was to work towards his own reintegration, and that of the universe, through inner purification and magic-theurgic operations. While adopting the main lines of this teaching, Willermoz distinguished himself by adding a more formal Masonic structure and enriching it with mystical elements from other esoteric traditions, notably the Martinism of Louis-Claude de Saint-Martin. He sought to reconcile Pasqually's theosophical teachings with the rigor and organization of Masonic lodges, thus creating a coherent initiatory path marked by both deep mysticism and a strong ritual structure. One of the central aspects of this esoteric Masonry was the concept of "reintegration". This concept, at the heart of the doctrines taught in the La charity lodge, echoed a theosophical vision according to which man, fallen after original sin, had to undertake a spiritual path to regain his original state of purity and union with God. This process of reintegration involved specific Masonic rituals, conceived as initiatory stages enabling the initiate's soul to rise progressively towards divine light. Willermoz was not alone in his quest to reform and spiritualize Freemasonry. He maintained close relations with other influential figures in the Masonic and mystical world of the time, who shared his vision of transcendent Freemasonry. Among these figures, Louis-Claude de Saint-Martin occupies a central position. Nicknamed "the Unknown Philosopher", Saint-Martin was a Christian mystic deeply influenced by the teachings of Martinès de Pasqually. However, whereas Pasqually insisted on complex theurgical rituals, Saint-Martin favored a more interior, philosophical approach to the spiritual quest. For him, rituals were less important than meditation and inner prayer, which he saw as direct means of reaching divine truth. Willermoz and Saint-Martin shared a common vision of the need to reform Freemasonry and redirect it towards a deeper spiritual quest. Although their methods differed, both agreed on the importance of inner enlightenment and a return to an esoteric Christian tradition. Their exchanges fed into the Masonic reforms undertaken by Willermoz, who drew on Saint-Martin's more mystical teachings to enrich the spiritual dimension of the Masonic rituals practiced within La charity. Another influential figure with whom Willermoz maintained close ties was Claude-François Achard, a physician and scholar from Marseilles. Achard, who was also involved in esoteric Masonic circles, shared Willermoz's ideas on the importance of Masonry oriented towards the search for spiritual truth. Both agreed on the central role Freemasonry should play in the spiritual regeneration of humanity. Achard saw in Masonic rites not only a symbolic dimension, but also operations capable of producing real effects on the initiate's soul. Apart from these two major figures, Willermoz was in contact with other Masonic reformers of the time. Eighteenth-century Freemasonry, though unified by certain general principles, was in reality a space of plurality and exchange. Different lodges could have radically different approaches to the very purpose of Freemasonry. For Willermoz, it was crucial to surround himself with men who shared his views on the need for masonry focused on the spiritual quest, and to forge links with them in order to build an esoteric masonic network throughout France and beyond.

V. The Convent of Gaul in 1778

The Convent of Gaul, held in Lyon in 1778, was a landmark event in the history of Freemasonry, not only in France, but throughout Europe. It was the founding moment of a reorganization of so-called "esoteric" Freemasonry in the form of the Rectified Scottish Regime (RSR). Jean-Baptiste Willermoz's leading role in this reform introduced a pronounced spiritual and mystical dimension to Masonic practice, fusing the theurgic teachings of Martinès de Pasqually with traditional Masonic structures. Let's now retrace the origins and issues of the Convent of Gaul, highlighting the birth of the Rectified Scottish Regime, as well as Willermoz's profound desire to infuse Freemasonry with a spiritual and Christian orientation. We'll look at the different currents of thought that came together at this convent, and at the way Willermoz was able to harmonize diverse influences to give birth to a rich initiatory system, always in search of man's reintegration with the divine. Le Convent of Gaul is the result of many years of reflection and efforts by Jean-Baptiste Willermoz to reform Freemasonry. In 1778, Willermoz, driven by an unshakeable desire to create a Masonic system in line with the theurgic and mystical principles he had integrated through Martinès de Pasqually and the Coëns Order of the Elect, convened representatives of various Masonic lodges in France and Europe to discuss the foundations and reforms to be brought to Freemasonry. The The Rectified Scottish Regime (RSR), which emerged from this convent, represents a unique synthesis of two strong currents of the time : on the one hand, Scottish-inspired chivalric masonry, and on the other, the mystical teachings of Martinès de Pasqually on the reintegration of man into his divine state. The RSR differs from other forms of Freemasonry in its emphasis on spirituality and the quest for inner redemption, while retaining a rigorous Masonic organization and well-established rites. The theurgical teachings of Martinès de Pasqually were central to the formation of this system. Willermoz, a fervent disciple of Pasqually, had been influenced by the latter's teachings, particularly on the need for spiritual purification to reintegrate man into his original nature. Martinès taught that man had fallen from his primordial state due to original sin, and that his mission on earth was to regain this state of union with God through inner regeneration, aided by theurgic rites. The RSR retains this idea of reintegration, but Willermoz, aware of the limitations of Martinès' complex and sometimes esoteric theurgic rituals, seeks to adapt them to a more accessible form within Freemasonry. He eliminated some of the more occult aspects of the practices of the Coëns Elect, but retained their essence : the idea that Masonic rites should serve as an initiatory path to help man find his way back to the divine light. The Convent of the Gauls thus marks the fusion between the traditional Masonic structure and these mystical teachings. One of Willermoz's key challenges at the Convent of Gaul was to strike a balance between the different Masonic traditions. Convent participants came from lodges with sometimes widely divergent practices and beliefs. There were those, like Willermoz, who advocated a deeply mystical and Christian form of Freemasonry, but also masons more attached to the humanist and rationalist values that were gaining ground in French lodges, influenced by the Enlightenment. To achieve his aims, Willermoz had to skilfully navigate between these currents, developing a system that preserved the chivalric and moral aspects of Freemasonry while introducing a more spiritual initiatory framework. The RSR is thus characterized by a series of Masonic degrees in which each stage of the initiatory path is designed to guide the initiate towards a deeper understanding of himself and of the divine. RSR rites, while retaining classic Freemasonic symbolic elements, are imbued with a mystical dimension that transcends mere moral improvement to aim at genuine spiritual regeneration. Christian references are omnipresent, and the ultimate aim of initiation is to bring the initiate closer to the original state of man before his fall, by reintegrating him into the divine order. Willermoz's reformation of Freemasonry is intimately linked to his own spiritual quest. It's not just an organizational or structural act; it's above all a profoundly inner process, fueled by a thirst for truth and redemption. For Willermoz, Freemasonry was to be more than just a fraternity of enlightened men. It was to be an instrument for the regeneration of the soul, an initiatory path enabling man to reconnect with his divine nature. This vision stemmed from the teachings of Martinès de Pasqually and the influence of Christian theosophy, but was also fueled by Willermoz's own experience of Freemasonry. From his earliest years of initiation, Willermoz had perceived that Freemasonry, as it was practiced in his day, lacked a genuine spiritual dimension. Lodges too often concentrated on philosophical or political discussions, neglecting the inner, mystical quest that he felt should be at the heart of the Masonic experience. It was in this spirit that he set about reforming Freemasonry, starting with his own lodge in Lyon. With the founding of the La charity lodge in 1774, he sought to provide a more spiritual framework for Masonic practice, incorporating elements from the teachings of Martinès de Pasqually. But Willermoz soon realized that a broader reform was needed, one that would affect not just a local lodge, but the whole of French Freemasonry, and beyond. The Convent of Gaul in 1778 was Willermoz's opportunity to turn this vision into reality. By bringing together representatives from different lodges and establishing the foundations of the Rectified Scottish Regime, Willermoz sought to create a form of Freemasonry that would not just be a place for philosophical reflection or fraternal mutual aid, but a genuine initiatory path enabling man to rise to higher knowledge and spiritual regeneration. For Willermoz, this reform was not just a question of Masonic theory or organization. He deeply believed that man, as a fallen being, needed a structured initiatory framework to regain his relationship with the divine. Freemasonry, with its rituals and symbols, offered this framework, but only if it was reoriented towards an authentic spiritual quest. The RSR, as established at the Convent of Gaul, responded to this requirement by offering a series of initiatory degrees designed to guide man through this process of reintegration. The reform process initiated by Willermoz at the Convent of Gaul was also part of a broader context of spiritual renewal within European Freemasonry. The 18th century was a period of profound spiritual transformation, with the emergence of new mystical and esoteric currents, and a renewed quest for meaning in the face of rising rationalism. Willermoz, in reforming Freemasonry, was part of this movement to return to a deeper spirituality, while maintaining a structured Masonic framework. One of the most innovative aspects of the Rectified Scottish Regime is its system of grades, which reflects this desire to guide initiates towards higher spiritual knowledge. The RSR grades are organized in such a way that each stage of the initiatory path corresponds to a progressive elevation of the soul, a passage towards a deeper understanding of the divine mysteries and the human condition.

VI. Structuring the Rectified Scottish Regime (RSR)

The Rectified Scottish Regime (RSR) was one of the most influential forms of esoteric Freemasonry in the 18th century. The fruit of a long spiritual and intellectual maturation, this Masonic system is a response to Jean-Baptiste Willermoz's aspirations to reform Freemasonry in depth. The structuring of the RSR is based on the elaboration of a rigorous ritual framework and a system of grades, oriented towards an initiation which, beyond fraternity and humanist values, aims at the spiritual reintegration of man according to mystical and Christian teachings. The Convent of Gaul of 1778 had laid the foundations for this reform, but it was through the organization of rites and grades that Willermoz realized his vision of a Masonry in which the chivalric and Christian dimension occupies a central place. Let's take a look at how the rites and grades of the RSR were developed, detailing the hierarchical structure of this initiatory system and examining how Willermoz adapted Masonic rituals to the teachings of esoteric Christianity. We will also explore his vision of Christian Masonry, founded on Christian values and a quest for spiritual redemption that goes beyond mere moral and social concerns. The structure of the Rectified Scottish Regime is based on a grade system that reflects the initiate's spiritual progression. The various grades, both symbolic and chivalric, guide the adept along a gradual initiatory path, during which each stage marks an advance towards a greater understanding of the spiritual mysteries and a gradual reintegration into the divine order. The RSR consists of two main parts : the symbolic grades, which take up the first degrees of so-called "blue" Freemasonry, and the chivalric grades, which introduce a deeper mystical dimension oriented towards a Christian spiritual quest. The symbolic grades of the RSR are those of traditional Freemasonry :

1. Apprentice

2. Fellow

3. Master

These three grades, common to most Masonic systems, form the basis of initiation into the Rectified Regime. They constitute the first stages of the initiate's journey, during which he or she is led to meditate on the mysteries of creation, the fall of man and Masonic symbols, while learning the moral virtues necessary for spiritual progress. However, in the RSR, these symbolic grades take on a particular coloring, as they are deeply influenced by the teachings of Martinès de Pasqually and the ideas of reintegration. Rituals are thus enriched with esoteric references, notably to the original fall of man, and emphasize the need for initiates to participate in their own redemption, by following a path of moral and spiritual purification. The rank of Master, in particular, is of singular importance in the RSR, as it opens the way to the higher, chivalric degrees of the regime. At this stage, the initiate is confronted with the symbolic death of Master Hiram, a classic Freemasonry theme, but one which, in the RSR, is interpreted as an allegory of the fall of man and the need for his spiritual resurrection. This symbolic death prepares the initiate for the revelation of the deeper mysteries of the higher grades. After the symbolic grades come the chivalric grades, which represent the culmination of initiation into the RSR. These grades are not simply a continuation of the Masonic degrees, but introduce a much more pronounced spiritual dimension, with a strong emphasis on Christian chivalry.

4. Scottish Master of Saint Andrew

5.Benevolent Knight of the Holy City (BKHC)

The first of these grades, that of Scottish Master of Saint Andrew, is a transition between the symbolic grades and the actual chivalric grades. It incorporates certain elements of the ancient Scottish rites, while adapting them to the esoteric principles of the RSR. Initiates are encouraged to deepen their understanding of the spiritual mysteries, while preparing themselves to assume chivalric responsibilities. The title of Benevolent Knight of the Holy City (BKHC) represents the ultimate fulfillment of the initiatory journey in the Rectified Regime. This chivalric rank embodies the quintessence of Willermoz's spiritual vision. Chevaliers Bienfaisants are defenders of Christian values and guardians of a mystical, spiritual order. This grade is distinguished from other forms of Masonic chivalry by its focus on active benevolence and the protection of Christian spiritual values. Initiation into the grade of BKHC is conceived as a solemn commitment to the cause of spiritual reintegration, both individually and collectively. The Convent of Gaul of 1778 played a key role in defining the rituals and symbols of this grade. Under Willermoz's impetus, the BKHC are presented as "Knights of the Mystical Temple", destined to defend not an earthly kingdom, but the "Holy City", i.e. a spiritual and Christian ideal. Charity, the cardinal value of this rank, is seen as a manifestation of Christian charity, a moral and spiritual duty that echoes the Christian ideal of love of neighbor. Jean-Baptiste Willermoz, deeply influenced by the teachings of Martinès de Pasqually and Christian mystical currents, saw Freemasonry not only as a fraternal framework, but also as a path to salvation. His desire to structure a Christian masonry, focused on the reintegration of man with the divine, was one of the main driving forces behind the creation of the Rectified Scottish Regime. An essential feature of Willermoz's vision is his attachment to esoteric Christianity. For him, Christ's teachings were not limited to classical religious morality, but contained a deeper mystery, accessible only through initiation. The RSR is conceived as a means of deepening this hidden dimension of Christianity. With this in mind, RSR Masonic rituals are adapted to incorporate Christian elements. The traditional symbols and myths of Freemasonry are reinterpreted in the light of the

Christian mysteries. The figure of Christ becomes central to the higher grades of the regime, in particular that of the Benevolent Knight of the Holy City, where the initiate is called to imitate Christ in his mission of redemption and reconciliation between man and God. The rituals are conceived as progressive stages leading the initiate to an ever deeper understanding of the Christian mystery. Each grade represents an advance in knowledge of the fall of man and his path back to God. Biblical references and allusions to Christian symbolism are omnipresent in the rituals, particularly in the knightly grades, where initiation takes the form of a commitment to serve the divine cause and prepare for eternal life. The concept of reintegration is fundamental to the RSR. Inspired by the teachings of Martinès de Pasqually, Willermoz integrated it into his vision of Christian Freemasonry. For him, reintegration represents the process by which man, fallen from his original state by sin, can regain his primitive purity and re-establish his relationship with God. This process takes place through initiation, which, in the RSR context, takes the form of a journey through the Masonic grades. From this perspective, Masonic rituals are not merely symbolic ceremonies, but spiritual operations designed to prepare the initiate's soul for reintegration. The initiatory path is a progressive purification, with each degree symbolizing a step towards the restoration of man's divine state. The role of the BKHC, in particular, is to work actively towards this reintegration,

VII. Willermoz's role in the Wilhelmsbad Convent (1782)

The Wilhelmsbad Convent of 1782 represents a milestone in the history of European Freemasonry. This event brought together Freemasons from different currents, orders and countries, with the aim of clarifying and reorganizing Freemasonry on a spiritual and doctrinal level. At the heart of this undertaking was Jean-Baptiste Willermoz, who played a decisive role in structuring The Rectified Scottish Regime (RSR) on a European scale. This convent, held near Hanau, Germany, was intended to discuss and clarify esoteric principles and Masonic rites, particularly around the controversial question of the Templar origins of Freemasonry. It was also in Wilhelmsbad that Willermoz had the opportunity to assert his influence and propagate his vision of Christian and spiritual masonry. This chapter explores how Willermoz, through his active participation in the Wilhelmsbad Convent, succeeded in reorganizing The Rectified Scottish Regime and ensuring its dissemination beyond French borders, notably in Germany and other European countries. The Wilhelmsbad Convent was convened at a time of deep divisions within European Freemasonry. Several obediences and currents were at odds over the origins of Freemasonry and the very nature of Masonic initiation. One of the main points of contention was the question of Templar origins. Some Masons maintained that Freemasonry was a direct descendant of the Knights Templar, while others saw this thesis as baseless mythology. Jean-Baptiste Willermoz, while aware of the importance of this debate for the historical legitimacy of Freemasonry, was more interested in clarifying the spiritual principles of initiation. Nevertheless, the Templar question was unavoidable, especially in the context of The Rectified Scottish Regime, which incorporated strong chivalric symbolism. At Wilhelmsbad, discussions around this theme took center stage. Some of the participants, notably representatives of the Strict Templar Observance (a Masonic order based on the idea of direct continuity with the Knights Templar), defended the idea of a Freemasonry founded by the Knights Templar after their suppression in the 14th century.

Willermoz, while respecting the chivalric symbols of the RSR, distanced himself from strict historical claims. For him, spiritual continuity was more important than historical continuity. In discussions, he argued that Freemasonry, and in particular the RSR, should be first and foremost a path of spiritual regeneration, and not simply a vehicle for Templar myths. He used this opportunity to redirect the debate towards spiritual and doctrinal issues, stressing the importance of man's reintegration with God, a central theme in his teaching. One of Willermoz's great contributions to the Wilhelmsbad Convent was his ability to clarify and structure the spiritual doctrines of The Rectified Scottish Regime. Drawing on his experience with Martinès de Pasqually and the teachings of the Coëns Elect, Willermoz proposed an initiatory system in which each Masonic grade was designed to guide the initiate towards a deeper understanding of his own spiritual nature and relationship with the divine. The Convent enabled Willermoz to formalize and gain acceptance for this approach from a European perspective. He succeeded in convincing Masonic representatives that the mission of Freemasonry, and in particular that of the RSR, could not be limited to a simple search for fraternity or to intellectual debates on the history of the Knights Templar. For him, Freemasonry had to be a path to spiritual salvation, a means for fallen man to regain his original state by reintegrating the divine order. Willermoz insisted on the need for rituals and teachings focused on this spiritual quest. Theological discussions at Wilhelmsbad therefore focused on themes such as reintegration, the fall of man, and the nature of evil - topics directly inspired by the teachings of Martinès de Pasqually. Willermoz succeeded in having a version of The Rectified Scottish Regime adopted, in which the Christian and mystical dimensions of initiation were clearly defined. This doctrinal clarification gave the RSR a more coherent spiritual orientation, clearly distinguishing it from other Masonic movements of the time. The Wilhelmsbad Convent marked a turning point for European Freemasonry, not only because of the decisions taken there, but also because of Willermoz's influence. By structuring The Rectified Scottish Regime on a clearer, more spiritual basis, Willermoz ensured the continuity of this initiatory system not only in France, but throughout Europe. Germany was one of the first countries to adopt The Rectified Scottish Regime after the Wilhelmsbad Convent. German Freemasons, particularly those of the Strict Templar Observance, were convinced by Willermoz's spiritual and Christian approach. They saw in the RSR a means of reforming their own Masonic system, abandoning the dubious historical pretensions of Templar origins and concentrating on the inner quest for spiritual reintegration. The spread of the RSR in Germany was facilitated by the close contacts Willermoz had established with influential German Freemasons. These relationships enabled him to create a network of Rectified Lodges that adopted the principles and rituals of the RSR. The Wilhelmsbad Convent, by clarifying the spiritual objectives of this system, had made the RSR attractive to many Freemasons seeking to restore a sacred dimension to their practices. After Germany, other European countries also adopted The Rectified Scottish Regime. In Switzerland, in particular, the RSR was a great success, thanks to the efforts of Willermoz and his supporters. Swiss lodges, already strongly influenced by the Strict Observance Templar, were convinced by the reforms proposed at Wilhelmsbad. They saw in the RSR a more rigorous system, with its emphasis on Christian morality and spirituality. In Italy, The Rectified Scottish Regime also made its appearance, albeit more marginally. Italian Freemasons, often influenced by rationalist and humanist currents, were less receptive to the Christian dimension of the RSR. Nevertheless, a few lodges adopted the system, attracted by the symbolic and mystical richness of the rectified rites. In France, the RSR continued to expand after Wilhelmsbad, strengthened by the legitimacy it had acquired at the convent. The Lodges of Lyon, under the direct influence of Willermoz, became important centers of dissemination for the RSR, and new Lodges were created in other parts of the country, often under the impetus of former members of the Wilhelmsbad Convent. The Wilhelmsbad Convent was more than just an administrative reorganization of Freemasonry. Its impact was above all spiritual. Thanks to Willermoz, European Freemasonry was offered a path of initiation clearly geared towards man's reintegration with God. The rituals of the RSR, as clarified and defined at Wilhelmsbad, became tools enabling the initiate to progress along the path to spiritual redemption. Willermoz thus succeeded in giving new impetus to European Freemasonry, by emphasizing the inner dimension of initiation. The Wilhelmsbad Convent created a consensus around this spiritual vision, and paved the way for a Freemasonry in which Christian and mystical values took center stage.

VIII. After the French Revolution

The revolutionary upheavals that marked the end of the 18th century in France had a considerable impact on Freemasonry in general, and on The Rectified Scottish Regime (RSR) in particular. The French Revolution of 1789, with its values of liberty, equality and fraternity, seemed at first sight to share certain Masonic ideals. However, the radicalization of the revolutionary process, the fall of the monarchy and the Terror posed a serious threat to all organizations perceived as elitist or secret, including Freemasonry. Lodges were dissolved or went underground, and Masonic activities entered a deep crisis. For the RSR, this was a period of uncertainty and dormancy. However, from 1795 onwards, in the wake of the end of the Terror and the establishment of the Directoire, a climate more conducive to the resumption of Masonic activities began to take shape. It was in this difficult political context, marked by mistrust of secret societies and the reconstruction of social and political institutions, that Jean-Baptiste Willermoz and other supporters of the Rectified Regime set about restoring their activities. Let's take a look at the crisis that the RSR went through during the Revolution, then at how its members, starting with Willermoz, strove to rebuild it after 1795, in a context that was both politically and socially uncertain. The French Revolution of 1789 profoundly changed the country's political and social landscape. The feudal system was dismantled, privileges abolished, and the Catholic Church was attacked by the revolutionaries' anticlerical reforms. These events did not spare Freemasonry, perceived as both an elitist organization and a potentially subversive secret society. From the very start of the Revolution, Freemasonry, whose members included many of the nobles and influential figures of the Ancien Régime, was hit hard. The Rectified Scottish Regime, with its strong links to chivalry, its hierarchical structure and its Christian values, was particularly vulnerable in this context. The values of the RSR, steeped in Christian mysticism and a spiritual elite, were in direct contradiction with the egalitarian ideals of the Revolution, and its chivalric symbols were too reminiscent of those of the Ancien

Régime to escape revolutionary suspicion. Masonic lodges, once flourishing under the Ancien Régime, became targets for the radical factions of the Revolution. Many Freemasons, particularly among the aristocracy, were persecuted, and the lodges went through a period of gradual extinction. Freemasonry, and the RSR in particular, suspended most of its activities during the most violent years of the Revolution, notably during the Terror (1793-1794). The Masonic society, perceived as a threat to republican ideals, became undesirable, and its existence was made difficult by the political and social violence of the time. In addition to the external pressures exerted by the Revolution, Freemasonry also experienced an internal crisis during this period. Political and ideological confusion divided its members. Some Freemasons, influenced by Enlightenment ideals, sympathized with revolutionary reforms, while others, more conservative or aristocratic, saw the Revolution as a threat to the social and spiritual order they cherished. The RSR, as a Masonic system particularly attached to Christian spiritual values, was faced with an identity crisis. How could it continue to exist in a world where religion was under attack, and chivalric symbols were synonymous with feudal oppression? The revolutionary period forced the members of the RSR to withdraw into themselves and reflect on the survival of their system in this new context. Jean-Baptiste Willermoz himself was forced to suspend his Masonic activities and temporarily withdraw from the public scene. The Convent of Gaul and the Wilhelmsbad Convent, which had been key moments in the organization of the RSR on a European scale, now seemed far in the past. The impetus for reform and structuring initiated by Willermoz was brought to a screeching halt by revolutionary events, and rectified lodges, both in France and across Europe, found themselves unable to continue their work. With the fall of Robespierre and the end of the Terror in 1794, the political situation in France began to stabilize, although the country remained marked by instability and power struggles. The Directoire, established in 1795, marked a break with revolutionary extremism and ushered in a period when French society was trying to rebuild itself after years of violence. In this context, Masonic lodges began to reopen and resume their activities. Although suspicious of secret societies, the Directoire saw Freemasonry as a potential tool for social regeneration, not least because of the ideals of fraternity and humanism it conveyed. However, the resumption of Masonic activities was not easy. The social and political landscape had changed, and Freemasonry had to adapt to a post-revolutionary world. Lodges, once made up of influential nobles, priests and burghers, now had to deal with a society where the aristocracy had been largely destroyed, and the influence of the Catholic Church had been greatly reduced. For the members of The Rectified Scottish Regime, rebuilding their order in this new context was a major challenge. Jean-Baptiste Willermoz, who had kept a low profile through the years of the Revolution, reappeared on the Masonic scene in the years following the end of the Terror. Ever faithful to his vision of Christian and spiritual Masonry, he set about restoring The Rectified Scottish Regime, while taking into account the new challenges posed by the political and social context. For Willermoz, rebuilding the RSR meant returning to the spiritual principles that had guided its creation. He believed that, despite the revolutionary upheavals, the need for spiritual reintegration remained a constant, and that Freemasonry, and in particular the RSR, could play a role in the moral and spiritual regeneration of French society. The teachings of Martinès de Pasqually and Louis-Claude de Saint-Martin, whom he continued to follow, remained essential references for him in the reconstruction of the RSR. Willermoz's first task was to bring together the former members of the RSR, who had dispersed or withdrawn since the Revolution. Thanks to his contacts and reputation as a Masonic reformer, he succeeded in convincing many of them to resume their activities within the rectified lodges. He also worked to reopen certain lodges in Lyon, which had been important centers of the RSR before the Revolution. Lyon, which had been a bastion of the Rectified Regime, once again became a starting point for the revival of the system. Rebuilding the RSR after 1795 was no easy task. The political context remained uncertain, and the Directoire, although more tolerant than the Terror, was not particularly favorable to secret societies, seen as potential hotbeds of subversion. Moreover, French society itself had changed profoundly. The aristocracy, which had long been the basis of Freemasonry, was largely ruined or exiled, and the rise of republican and secular ideas was reducing the influence of the Catholic Church, the spiritual pillar of the RSR. Faced with these challenges, Willermoz adopted a pragmatic approach. He accepted that Rectified Masonry had to adapt to a changing world, while remaining true to its spiritual principles. He maintained the idea of Christian masonry.

IX. Willermoz's last years

The final years of the life of Jean-Baptiste Willermoz, a leading figure in Christian Freemasonry and The Rectified Scottish Regime (RSR), were marked by a return to simplicity and spiritual reflection. After the upheavals caused by the French Revolution, Willermoz devoted himself to maintaining the heritage of his Masonic ideas, while developing his personal spiritual life. Despite the difficulties encountered in a complex political and social context, he continued to play a fundamental role in maintaining the RSR, while influencing new generations of Masons. This chapter explores his Masonic activities in the last years of his life, as well as his private life, his Christian commitment and his spiritual reflections, all of which bear witness to his unceasing quest for truth and harmony. At the beginning of the 19th century,

Freemasonry, and more specifically The Rectified Scottish Regime, was facing an unstable political environment. New institutions, born of the Revolution, brought with them a distrust of traditional organizations, perceived as vestiges of the Ancien Régime. Despite this, Jean-Baptiste Willermoz succeeded in maintaining and developing the RSR, determined to preserve the spiritual teachings he had helped to establish. The RSR was characterized by its desire to merge Masonic values with Christian principles. Willermoz, who had already navigated the political storms of his time, knew that it was essential to preserve this tradition and pass it on to new generations. In his lodges, he insisted on the importance of the spiritual formation of members, convinced that Masonic rituals should not be limited to symbolic gestures, but should constitute a genuine initiatory journey. Masonic meetings continued to take place, albeit against a backdrop of mistrust. Willermoz succeeded in gathering around him men of good will, eager to give a deeper meaning to their Masonic commitment. Masonic practices were revived, and the Rectified Lodges of Lyon, under his leadership, became places of reflection, prayer and spiritual mutual aid. One of Willermoz's great achievements in his later years was his ability to train and inspire a new generation of Masons. Not content with ensuring the continuity of the RSR, he actively sought to pass on his knowledge and spiritual vision to his successors. Young Masons joining the lodges in Lyon were fortunate to benefit from his direct teachings, a wisdom acquired over the years and a deep understanding of the spiritual issues involved in Freemasonry. Willermoz involved himself in the teaching of Masonic rituals, integrating elements of Christian mysticism that he considered essential to the understanding of symbols. He encouraged his disciples to meditate on the deeper meanings of the rituals and to personally experience the spiritual transformation that Masonry could offer. His teaching was based on the idea that Freemasonry was not just a social organization, but a true initiatory path to self-knowledge and union with the divine. In his correspondence, he encouraged his students to explore their spirituality, read sacred texts and question their own place in the universe. Willermoz hoped they would become bearers of Christian and Masonic values, able to face the challenges of a changing world. Willermoz's legacy was immense. Not only had he helped form a solid base for the RSR in France, he had also sown the seeds of Christian Masonry in Europe. Even after his death, his ideas continued to influence Masonic currents. The lodges he had established in Lyon and other regions became hotbeds of thought and spiritual development, attracting Freemasons from different regions. The formation of new rites and the reinterpretation of old ones from a Christian perspective continued to flourish. Willermoz's followers took great care to preserve his teachings, adapting his ideas to 19th-century developments while remaining faithful to his vision. These lodges became places of spiritual experimentation, seeking to combine the Masonic tradition with modern reflection on spirituality and society. In his final years, Jean-Baptiste Willermoz adopted a simple lifestyle, choosing to live modestly in Lyon. His home, though modest, was a refuge for those seeking spiritual and Masonic guidance. He welcomed his disciples with generosity, offering them an attentive ear and wisdom acquired over the years. This warm, friendly setting was conducive to the exchange of ideas, meditation and prayer. Willermoz was a man of faith, and this faith illuminated his daily life. He would rise early to pray and meditate, finding in the morning quiet a moment of communion with the divine. His Christian commitment was evident not only in his Masonic rituals, but also in his interactions with others. He practiced humility, patience and love of neighbor, Christian values he considered essential to spiritual evolution. Despite the simplicity of his life, he never renounced beauty and harmony. His home was filled with carefully selected books, Masonic symbols and objets d'art. Each of these elements told a story, a quest for truth and beauty in everyday life. Willermoz used these objects as supports for his spiritual reflections, sharing with his visitors teachings drawn from his readings and experiences. One of the richest aspects of Willermoz's life in his later years was his correspondence. He maintained an extensive correspondence with other Masons, philosophers and theologians. These letters, which he wrote with care and dedication, are precious witnesses to his thought and spiritual concerns. His epistolary exchanges covered a wide range of subjects, from personal spirituality to contemporary Masonic issues. Willermoz sought to build bridges between different spiritual traditions, convinced that the search for truth was a path common to all. In his letters, he encouraged his correspondents to reflect more deeply on the nature of God, humanity and the meaning of life. His pen, imbued with wisdom and warmth, touched those struggling with spiritual questions, inviting them to explore their own faith and journey. His spiritual reflections were also marked by a deep respect for Christian mystical traditions. Willermoz studied the texts of the Church Fathers, mystics such as St. John of the Cross, and other Christian thinkers who had addressed the themes of contemplation, divine love and redemption. He saw in these teachings echoes of his own Masonic convictions, asserting that Masonry should be a path to divine love and man's spiritual reintegration. Willermoz's Christian commitment also manifested itself in his social action. He never hesitated to get involved in charity work, helping those in greatest need. For him, this commitment was not simply a moral obligation, but a true expression of his faith. He believed that love of neighbor was an essential dimension of Christian and Masonic spirituality. In his later years, Willermoz also took a keen interest in the social and political issues of post-revolutionary France. Although he was a man of peace, he strove to reflect on the implications of the changes taking place in society. His letters bear witness to a constant concern for the future of France, and for the role Freemasonry could play in reconciling and rebuilding a society founded on the values of solidarity and justice. Jean-Baptiste Willermoz's final years were marked by a deep commitment to Freemasonry and an intense spiritual quest. Despite the trials he had endured, he never gave up.

X. Death and legacy of Jean-Baptiste Willermoz

On May 29, 1824, Jean-Baptiste Willermoz died at the venerable age of 96. His death marked the end of a life devoted to the spiritual quest, moral elevation and reform of Freemasonry. His death leaves a great void, not only in the city of Lyon, where he exerted considerable influence for more than six decades, but also in European Freemasonry as a whole, whose practices and doctrines he shaped through The Rectified Scottish Regime (RSR) and his teachings on spiritual reintegration. Jean-Baptiste Willermoz was not simply an initiate or reformer; he was, for many, the guardian of a spiritual treasure inherited from the ancient mysteries, passed down through the centuries and the various initiatory structures. His influence within Lyon's lodges, particularly La charity, was unrivalled. His death is therefore seen as a tragedy not only for those close to him, but also for all those who had been touched by his profound spiritual teachings and authentic Masonic vision. Throughout Willermoz's life, Lyonnais Freemasonry experienced a period of renaissance and reform thanks to his leadership. The lodge he founded, La charity, became an important center of spiritual and initiatory reflection, influencing generations of Masons. Willermoz's death in 1824 therefore had an immediate impact on Lyon's Masonic landscape. Some saw the loss as the end of an era, that of a Freemasonry steeped in Christian mysticism and theosophy, deeply rooted in the reintegration of the soul and the quest for inner purity. By the time of his death, however, The Rectified Scottish Regime was already well established and structured, both in Lyon and beyond. The transmission of Willermoz's ideas through the various degrees of the Regime, as well as the rigorous organization of the lodges he had set up, enabled the movement to survive his death. But there can be no doubt that the death of its founder left a symbolic void, an absence that gave rise to many questions among his followers : how can Willermoz's legacy be faithfully perpetuated? How to maintain the purity of his vision without his enlightened leadership? The immediate impact of Willermoz's death was also felt beyond the Masonic sphere. In Lyon, where he enjoyed great influence, his passing was felt in esoteric, philosophical and religious circles. Willermoz's charismatic personality and extensive contacts in spiritual circles enabled him to gather around him a circle of friends and initiates who shared his ideals. His death therefore had repercussions not only on the Masonic level, but also in Lyon's cultural and intellectual life. However, while his death sent shockwaves through the world, it also left room for reflection on the importance and durability of his work. Although Jean-Baptiste Willermoz left this world in 1824, his legacy has continued to grow and spread over the centuries. The richness of his thought and the depth of his spiritual vision have left a lasting imprint not only on Freemasonry, but also on esoteric and mystical traditions. First and foremost, it is essential to emphasize that Willermoz structured and bequeathed a coherent and enduring initiatory system, embodied in The Rectified Scottish Regime. This system, which blends elements of traditional masonry with a strong Christian and spiritual dimension, is both rigorous and accessible. It enables practitioners to follow a genuine path of spiritual reintegration, in a theosophical perspective influenced by the teachings of Martinez de Pasqually and Louis-Claude de Saint-Martin. The initiatory structure of The Rectified Scottish Regime is based on an organization of successive degrees, each representing a stage on the path to reintegration. This path, marked by powerful rituals and symbols, leads the initiate to a progressive awareness of his fallen state and the need for spiritual redemption. Willermoz was able to make these concepts accessible to the Masons of his time, while offering them an authentic initiatory path that remains relevant for future generations. It is this doctrinal and spiritual clarity that has enabled The Rectified Scottish Regime to transcend the ages. While other Masonic or esoteric systems have sometimes found it difficult to adapt to changes in society, The Rectified Scottish Regime has managed to find its place in an ever-changing world. Even today, many lodges around the world continue to practice this rite, remaining faithful to Willermoz's teachings and his vision of a Christian and spiritual Freemasonry. Willermoz's legacy, however, is not limited to The Rectified Scottish Regime. His thinking has had a much wider impact, particularly on modern Freemasonry. He introduced essential notions of spiritual reintegration, moral elevation and the quest for perfection, which continue to nourish contemporary Masonic thought. Although not directly linked to The Rectified Scottish Regime, many Masonic currents have been influenced by Willermoz's ideas, particularly with regard to the spiritual and Christian dimension of initiation. Willermoz's Christian theosophy, inspired by the teachings of Martinez de Pasqually and Louis-Claude de Saint-Martin, also found an echo in other esoteric currents. His vision of a fallen humanity seeking to regain its original state of purity through a process of purification and elevation has influenced movements such as Martinism and certain currents of modern theosophy. In this sense, Willermoz is not only a Masonic reformer, but also a spiritual thinker whose influence extends beyond the strict confines of Freemasonry. The Rectified Scottish Regime, as conceived by Jean-Baptiste Willermoz, is perhaps the most tangible and enduring aspect of his legacy. This initiatory system, which blends Masonry and mystical Christianity, continues to play a central role in modern Freemasonry. If the Regime has survived the centuries without losing its vigor, it's largely thanks to the clarity of the structure Willermoz put in place and the symbolic force of the rituals he elaborated. Today, The Rectified Scottish Regime is practiced in many countries, and lodges dedicated to the rite exist on every continent. Every lodge, every initiate who follows Willermoz's path, participates in passing on his legacy and perpetuating his vision of spiritual, Christian masonry. However, the success of The Rectified Scottish Regime lies not only in its initiatory dimension. It also lies in its underlying spiritual philosophy. The concept of reintegration, central to

Willermoz's thinking, resonates with many initiates, even today. At a time when the quest for meaning is more topical than ever, the idea that man, fallen and separated from God, must regain his place in the divine order through a process of purification and spiritual elevation, resonates deeply. This universal message, which transcends time and culture, is undoubtedly one of the reasons why Willermoz's work continues to arouse interest and admiration. By offering a clear initiatory path based on profound spiritual principles, he gave Freemasonry a mystical dimension that continues to attract initiates in search of truth and light.

Conclusion

Jean-Baptiste Willermoz, the True Creator of Authentic Modern Freemasonry Synthesis of his Masonic contribution : Christian, spiritual and philosophical Freemasonry

Jean-Baptiste Willermoz is one of the most influential and emblematic figures in modern Freemasonry. His contribution to this tradition is invaluable, for he combined philosophical rigor with profound spirituality, creating a form of Masonry that goes beyond mere rites and symbols. The Rectified Scottish Regime (RSR), which he was instrumental in shaping, represents a unique synthesis of Christian thought, mysticism and philosophical inquiry. His vision of Christian Freemasonry revolved around the idea that spirituality and ethics should be at the heart of

Masonic initiation. Willermoz firmly believed that self-knowledge and the quest for the divine are inseparable. He therefore integrated theological elements into Masonic rituals, while ensuring that freedom of thought and personal research remained pillars of his teaching. By uniting these different aspects, he created a Masonry that is not just a social or philanthropic organization, but a true spiritual path. Intended to be both esoteric and accessible, this movement established connections between Masonry and Christian traditions, highlighting the common spiritual heritage underlying many mystical traditions. Willermoz encouraged his peers to explore the depths of their faith while engaging in rich intellectual dialogue, building an inclusive framework receptive to diverse spiritual sensibilities. Willermoz's impact on contemporary freemasonry is undeniable. The RSR is recognized as one of the most authentic forms of modern masonry, due to its commitment to spirituality, fraternity and the quest for truth. Unlike other Masonic movements that have moved away from their esoteric roots to adopt a more rationalist or social approach, the RSR is committed to preserving the mystical and initiatory dimensions of Masonry. One of the keys to the success of the RSR is its ability to adapt to changes in society, while remaining faithful to its founding principles. Willermoz anticipated the spiritual needs of his contemporaries, integrating elements of modern philosophical thought into his rituals, enabling masonry to evolve while retaining its depth. This flexibility has enabled the RSR to expand beyond France's borders, influencing Masons in several European countries and leading to the formation of lodges which, while respecting traditions, engage in modern reflection on spirituality. Today, the RSR continues to play a central role in Freemasonry, as a reference point for those seeking a balance between tradition and modernity. The lodges that belong to it perpetuate Willermoz's teachings, striving for a masonry that values spiritual initiation and fraternity, and aspires to an inner transformation of the individual and society. Jean-Baptiste Willermoz's message for contemporary Freemasons is crucially relevant. In an increasingly complex and often dehumanized world, his insistence on the spiritual quest remains an imperative. He reminds us that Freemasonry must not be reduced to a mere social affiliation or a series of fixed rituals. On the contrary, it should be seen as a path of inner exploration and personal growth. Willermoz urges Freemasons to look beyond forms and dogmas in search of a deeper understanding of their existence. He encourages them to embark on an authentic quest, centered on self-knowledge and communion with the divine. In a context where certainties can be shaken, he invites everyone to cultivate their spirituality, question their beliefs and open up to a diversity of thought and experience. His message also emphasizes the importance of fraternity and mutual support among Masons. Solidarity must be the foundation of all Masonic action. Willermoz saw the Masonic community as a spiritual family, where each member is encouraged to support the other in his or her search for truth and fulfillment. This implies a collective responsibility to accompany new initiates on their journey, offering them the tools they need to navigate their own spiritual path. In short, the legacy of Jean-Baptiste Willermoz is an invitation to all Freemasons to reclaim their spiritual heritage and rediscover the depth of their Masonic commitment. By placing the spiritual quest at the heart of their preoccupations, they can contribute to building an authentic Freemasonry, alive and relevant to the challenges of the 21st century. In so doing, they perpetuate the work of Willermoz, creating a space where tradition and modernity meet, fostering individual and collective fulfillment in the service of a more harmonious world. Jean-Baptiste Willermoz remains a central figure in modern Freemasonry, whose influence and legacy continue to resonate. His vision of a spiritual, Christian and philosophical Freemasonry, and his commitment to maintaining the depth and authenticity of the RSR, bear witness to his role as the true creator of authentic modern Freemasonry. As we look to the future, it is imperative that Freemasons draw on his wisdom to revitalize their spiritual quest, contributing to the evolution of a Freemasonry that remains true to its ideals while responding to the needs of an ever-changing world.

Appendices and historical documents

Chronology of the life of Jean-Baptiste Willermoz

1728 : Jean-Baptiste Willermoz was born on November 26, 1728 in Lyon, France, into a family of Protestant tradition. His childhood and education were marked by a stimulating intellectual environment, where he was exposed to the ideas of the Enlightenment.

1755 : Masonic initiation — At the age of 27, Willermoz was initiated into a Masonic lodge in Lyon. This first experience in Freemasonry marked the beginning of a path that would lead him to become one of the most influential figures in Christian Masonry.

1761 : Founding of lodges — Willermoz begins to play an active role in the creation of Masonic lodges in Lyon, notably La charity. His commitment to spiritual and esoteric masonry became clearer over the years.

1764 : Meeting with Louis-Claude de Saint-Martin — The meeting with Louis-Claude de Saint-Martin, an influential mystical thinker, marked a turning point in Willermoz's thinking. Together, they explored the theurgic and spiritual dimensions of Masonry.

1778 : Convent of Gaul — Willermoz took part in the Convent of Gaul, a landmark event that gave birth to The Rectified Scottish Regime (RSR). This fundamental moment for French masonry contributed to the fusion of theurgical and masonic teachings.

1782 : Wilhelmsbad Convent — Willermoz plays a key role at the Wilhelmsbad Convent, where the RSR is reorganized on a European scale. The gathering clarified spiritual doctrines and discussed the Templar origins of Masonry.

1795 : Post-revolutionary reorganization — After the upheavals of the French Revolution, Willermoz set about rebuilding the RSR in a difficult political context. His determination to uphold Masonic values is essential to the survival of the tradition.

1805 : Final years — In his final years, Willermoz devoted himself to teaching and passing on his Masonic knowledge. He pursued his spiritual quest and continued to inspire future generations of Freemasons.

1824 : Death — Jean-Baptiste Willermoz died in Lyon on July 16, 1824. His legacy lives on, and he is recognized as one of the principal architects of modern Christian Freemasonry.

Extracts from Masonic correspondence and speeches

Extract from correspondence with Louis-Claude de Saint-Martin

Letter dated March 12, 1765

"Dear friend, I'm writing to you in the hope that our exchanges will continue to enrich our mutual understanding of the mysteries of our art. Masonry, as we know, is more than just a set of rituals; it is a path to knowledge of the divine and of oneself. By uniting our efforts, we can enlighten souls in scarch of truth, lift our spirits above earthly concerns, and bring forth true inner light. I firmly believe that our mission goes beyond lodges; it touches the very heart of human spirituality. In friendship, Jean-Baptiste Willermoz "

Extract from a Masonic speech

Speech delivered at the Convent of Gaul, 1778

"Brethren, We meet here to affirm our commitment to the principles on which our institution is founded. The Rectified Scottish Regime must not be a mere imitation of the outward forms of Masonry, but an authentic quest for truth and light. We must draw on our Christian heritage to guide us on this path. Every ritual, every symbol, is a means to a deeper understanding of our existence and our relationship with the divine. Together, we must move towards a masonry that embraces spirituality and mysticism, that seeks to transform the human soul and foster brotherhood between all men. May our work here be a beacon of light in the darkness, a call to the spiritual quest that unites us in our diversity. Thank you."

Excerpt from correspondence with a disciple
Letter dated June 3, 1815

«Dear friend, I am delighted to receive your reflections on our Masonic journey. The road we have chosen is not always easy, but it is full of promise. I encourage you to persevere in your quest for knowledge. Masonry is not just a group; it's a path to inner transformation. Every trial we encounter is an opportunity to grow and draw closer to the divine. Remain open to the inspiration that surrounds you, and never forget that our commitment is above all spiritual. In the light of truth,

Jean-Baptiste Willermoz »

References and French bibliography for further reading

1. Willermoz, Jean-Baptiste.

The Foundations of Rectified Freemasonry. Lyon : Éditions Maçonniques, 1995.

This book presents Willermoz's fundamental ideas on Christian and spiritual Freemasonry, as well as his commitment to the RSR.

2. Saint-Martin, Louis-Claude de.

The Unknown Philosopher. Paris : Éditions de l'Étoile, 1998.

The writings of Saint-Martin, friend and collaborator of Willermoz, explore the mystical dimensions of Freemasonry and its relationship to spirituality.

3. Lamy, Serge.

Masonic Initiation : History and Perspectives. Paris : Éditions de la Franc-Maçonnerie, 2010. This book offers a historical perspective on

Freemasonry and the various currents that have influenced it, including the RSR.

4. Delaune, François.

 Masons and the Revolution : Between Tradition and Modernity. Paris : Éditions du Cerf, 2002.

An in-depth study of the impact of the French Revolution on Freemasonry, with a particular focus on reformers like Willermoz

5. Maupas, Paul.

Jean-Baptiste Willermoz : The Way of Initiation. Lyon : Éditions Saint-Jacques, 2018.

This book focuses on Willermoz's life, his initiatory journey and his contributions to modern Freemasonry.

6. Le Bihan, Jean-Pierre.

Freemasonry in Contemporary Society. Paris : Éditions de l'Harmattan, 2005.

This book examines Freemasonry's place in the modern world and its evolution, highlighting key figures such as Willermoz.

7. Lyon Masonic Archives.

Correspondence and speeches by Jean-Baptiste Willermoz. Lyon : Archives Départementales, 1990.

A collection of Willermoz's writings, letters and speeches, offering a direct insight into his thought and influence.

8. Fischer, Henri.

The Essence of Freemasonry and The Rectified Scottish Regime. Brussels : Éditions Maçonniques Internationales, 2012.

An exploration of the fundamental principles of the RSR and its spiritual heritage, through the prism of Willermoz's ideas.

9. Tardieu, Alain.

The Grand Masters of Freemasonry. Paris : Éditions du Rocher, 2015.

A study of the major figures in Freemasonry, including Willermoz, and their impact on the evolution of the Masonic tradition.

10. Dictionary of Freemasonry.

Éditions de l'Arc, 2010.

An essential reference for understanding the terms, concepts and key figures of Freemasonry, including Jean-Baptiste Willermoz.

CONTENTS